Glimmers of Hope

Anagha Pratheep

BookLeaf
Publishing

India | USA | UK

Glimmers of Hope © 2023 Anagha Pratheep

All rights reserved.

Presentation by *BookLeaf Publishing*

Web: www.bookleafpub.com

E-mail: info@bookleafpub.com

ISBN: 9789358735222

First edition 2023

To everyone hoping that life gets better, because it does and you'll be so glad that you held on.

ACKNOWLEDGEMENT

I want to take this opportunity to thank my parents for supporting my wild dreams, my friends for encouraging me(to go for things even when I'm scared to follow through with them), and my cousins for being the first ones I shared these poems with.

A special thank you to Isabella, my therapist, for helping me see the light when I felt like giving it all up.

And an infinite thankyou to Felix,my little cat, for being there for me.
I love you all so much.

Also this wouldn't be my book if I didn't start off by shouting out my favorite artists who have been there with me through all the highs and lows: Taylor Swift I love you Evermore and BTS thank you for helping me find that Magic Shop when I need it- which is always.

PREFACE

Hello! Thank you for picking up this book and giving it a chance. These are poems that I wrote throughout the years. I hope you can relate to these poems- daydreams, heartbreaks, I'd write it all down. And I promise that even when you feel like there's no hope and you're at your breaking point... you'll find that Glimmer of Hope soon enough.

The Place You'll Find Me

A place where the blue pristine water hits the
rocky pebble shore and presents it with respite
from the hurricanes of life

A place where the flutter of butterfly wings
makes a ripple strong enough to move the largest
mountain

A place where fallen autumn leaves turn into a
solace for little critters hoping to be shielded
from the first specks of snow fall

A place where every hurdle you've ever faced is
wrapped up into a tiny shining orb and floats
down a choppy river, so you never feel pain
again

Where lilac hyacinths spring up from the
despondent snow ready for clandestine meetings
with the golden sun

Where tiny fireflies , flying around, illuminate
the darkest nights searching for something one
can only describe as love

Where everything you are afraid of leads you
back to who you really are
Where you find that light that only shines once
in a lifetime
That's where you'll find me surrounded by
glimmers of hope

Where even a glimpse of your face in the broken
mirror shows you the infinite potential that hides
within

A place where even the smallest embers make
beautiful fires that keep you warm
A place where things fall apart only to be
brought back together in ways that are infinitely
bewitching
That's where you'll find me

Finding Lost Hope

I once hid in the shadows
Afraid of what would happen if I turned my face
to see the rainbow reflections of suncatchers in
the window on a summer afternoon

The natural ebullience of young children without
a care in the world
I wish I could close my eyes and disappear into
that world again
Even if it was just for a moment

Back when zeal dictated my every move instead
of fears of falling and failing and disappearing
into oblivion
Back when I believed in myself and everyone
believed in me
Back when I saw the good in everyone and
thought no one would ever hurt me

Naïve, nonchalant you can call it what you want
I miss those days filled with rainbow reflections
and golden glimmers of a bright future

Fell off the ladder of the path I climbed my
whole life for

Somewhere somehow I became used to the
misery
Found the darkness engulfing me like a warm
blanket after a day swimming in the cold sea
Hiding in a cave of only pain

In my dreams, I slowly turn toward the light
Watch the shadows of the past disappear as
I see the specks of the iridescent glow of the
future

I wake and realize that maybe for once
Not all hope is lost

Appearances

I'm scared this will end like it did in the past
Empty faces mocking me
Just because I'm not more like them

I would have done anything to trade my curly
locks for pin-straight hair
If I could have been a bit taller
Had a slimmer frame maybe they'd like me
more then
So I'd go home starve my body, stand on the
scale, and watch the numbers go down just like
my self-esteem- that they walked all over

Maybe if I wasn't so quiet
Maybe if I wasn't clumsy
Maybe then they'd like me more
Maybe I'd like me more

Never was a fan of my face
Brown orbs the color of a mocha latte that I
don't even like the taste of
All these marks and indentations
Scars I don't want to see
Appearances I would keep up just to save face
Make them believe I didn't hate me

I spent years painting on layers of makeup
Hoping it would mask how I really see myself
Hating who I really was
Every mirror I avoided

It took years but for the first time it is clear to
me
I was trying to fix things that didn't need fixing
An impossible task, I thought I could possibly
figure out

It's not my face or body that needed fixing
It is my mind
Blinded by comparisons
It's time to embrace all my colors, even the ones
I don't particularly like

This time when I see my face in the mirror
I see my brown eyes and thank them for how
they catch the glimmers of sunlight
I see my broad shoulders and remind myself I
can win any fight
This time I see myself as more than just who I
look like
Because truth be told there's so much more to
me than appearances

Just Kids

When we were younger we'd play dress up in
my room
Silly dolls and dreaming up a life we could only
yearn for
You'd hold my hand and we'd annihilate the
monsters who came out at night
We'd save each other in every scenario we made
up
Explored our backyard thinking it was some
faraway land where nothing could ever hurt us

I'd daydream of a prince coming to save me
Riding off into a sunset
Happily ever after that's what I believed in
Back when I thought anything was possible

I'd grab your arm every time I was scared when
the clowns would come out in scary movies
Because only you could calm my fears
Back when I thought the scariest thing was a
monster on a screen
Now we laugh at scary movies because real life
is more sinister than anything else

We'd meet in the meadows

Surrounded by a million wildflowers
We'd pick flowers and make potions that could
save the world
Talk about the adventures we'd go on when
we're older

The voices that told us what to be and how to act
We'd block them all out, back when we weren't
afraid of letting anyone down

I wonder if you miss those days because I do
I miss when my worries didn't keep me up at
night
I miss when I didn't know about responsibilities
No bills to pay just some kids lost in their own
daydreams
Wishing we could grow up and make them
realities

I miss when those older than us had solutions to
everything
I miss when I looked at life with rose-tinted
glasses
Everything had an silver lining

I once thought our parents were perfect
How could they not be?
Took me a while to learn no one is an invincible
superhero

Like us, they're only human
Deep down we're all just kids who were forced
to grow up

Too Much

You look in my eyes
Compare them to a pretty sunrise
Surrounded in the dark by a million twinkling
fireflies
Everything felt so right with you
But nothing lasts forever
Maybe I just burn too bright
Something about being blinding

I dreamt of Sunday mornings
Where we'd sleep in
Even when it was storming, we'd find sweet
shelter in each other
Call it a missing puzzle piece
I knew you wanted me the first time we locked
eyes
Classic, I'm almost scared to call it because
what are two kids at 23 supposed to know

I was the life of the party
You loved how I wrapped them around me
No one could be free from my spell
And soon enough you fell

At least that's what you told everyone before
you took my sparkles away
And suddenly you don't like the way I sound
And I'm too loud
And you hate my laugh
And then you say my taste in music is maimed
I need to throw out all the things I love
My dreams are too ambitious
And suddenly I'm too much all at once for you
Too focused, too driven, just too in love with
you, and apparently that's all too much

I guess girls like me are only fun to see from a
distance
The idea of them, nice and kind and they treat
you right that's all great
But if they speak their own mind, turn away
from listening to your every word and ask for
equity
now that's the most heinous crime
And I see now that I'm not who you want
because I'm too much
So please go find less

Missing You

Maybe I took it all for granted
I guess they were right when they say you don't
know how much someone means to you until
they're gone
Flew in the sky and still didn't appreciate the
way the marshmallow clouds engulfed me in a
warm embrace
Something like hot cocoa on a winter day

Maybe I could've taken a snapshot in time
Memorized your voice and how your dimples
nestled into your cheek every time you smiled
The smell of the ocean breeze as you convinced
me to get in the water
The silly jokes that you cracked, made me roll
my eyes and look away
I should have taken it all in because I didn't
realize everything I once believed would last
forever would be taken away

I always thought I'd see you again
I thought for some reason I'd have more time
with you
Didn't know the days were numbered
Breaking like a string trying to hold us together

Wish I learned more about your favorite things
Took more pictures of our moments
Because time stole you away and even when I
begged you to stay
Fate still took you away

Maybe I was being delusional
Hoping that this was destiny
That I had more time with you
Because I know not to believe in forever but
with you forever seemed to not be enough time
I went home and begged every celestial force to
just let us be
Convinced myself I'd be enough for you

The message in the silence
It's clearer than the way my heart used to beat
for you
I'm not going to lie, I'm not innocent
I hope you know that I miss you though

For You

I'm looking at you through neon lighting
Knowing you're the only reason I
Keep fighting

If I could tell you
I would
I'd let you know
You saved me
When I was at my lowest
And you don't even know it
You're the reason I keep going
Even when I'm breaking and crying

I get back up
Only because I know I'll do anything
To make it
To tell you that I made it because of you

You smile and I can't look away
You might be oceans away
But you're still the only one who makes me
smile
The only one who makes me believe in dreams

I can't without you

So when you pull me onto your chest
Sing me those songs... I'll know I deserve it
When I'm with you
I'm home
Looking in your raven eyes
Nothing could be better

I'd do anything you want me to do
I know you want success
So I chase it

The End

Goodbyes broken ties
I'm paralyzed with fear
I don't want to lose you
Don't need this to end like my worst fears
I'm your decalcomania so shape me any way
you please

Bruises on my skin
From the demons, you brought back in
They keep coming back
Where do I go from here

You're gone and I'm just standing here
Peering into the empty rooms
Left out in the cold
Watch everyone move on
Forget everything about me
Fading into oblivion

Fall down to the flames one more time
Turn my soul into ashes to be reborn again
Throw it all out
Start from the rubble
Claim I'm a Phenoix
Is that what I need to do

An earthquake to my soul
A shock wave to my dignity
Will that save me

There's only so many times I can rise from the
flames
Is this the last time
I'm getting tired of this game I play with myself
How many second chances do you give yourself
when all you feel is broken
I guess I don't have a choice
Other than to sit with myself

Here we go again I'll dust myself off
Show off my new battle wounds

I'm done
shaping myself into who you want me to be
I'm no longer clay in your hands waiting for you
to mold me in anyway you please

No matter how hard I try
It's just me in the end
And nothing I say or do will make you stay
So I'll build myself up again, but this time I
won't do it for you
I'm doing this for me

Wish I Never Met You

I kept my distance
Scared that I'd get sucked into the whirlpool
I should've known this would have ended like
this

You held the door open
I opened my own door trying to avoid you
You asked me about my dreams
You kept trying so I let you in

I've never heard warning sirens the way they
went off in my head
Red and blue lights go off in the rear view
mirror
I've never been so afraid
Never felt so small
My hands still shake when I think of you

I sit alone and wish I never met you
I wish you never trapped me in between your
arms
Took my wings and tore them off
Leaving broken feathers to sink down

Years later I bet you don't even remember, but I
do
I didn't know what to say then
I was speechless
Too young to understand your true intentions
Too young to know the truth
Why do all the demons that visit me in my
nightmares share your face

There's no cold hard proof
There's no marks you can see
No body, no crime that's what they say
But even if you don't know it, you've left scars
in my mind that only I see
Wish I knew what I knew now because I would
never let you get away with it

Fight, Flight and Freeze

I always had this fantasy
I once believed it would become a reality
That years later you wouldn't have the same
power over me
No fight, flight, and freeze every time you lay
your remorseless eyes on me

I remember the nights when you'd crawl into my
dreams
Begging for attention and feeding off my fear
like a villain in a movie
Sweat dripped down my back, and I would wake
up in a panic
I thought those days were finally over

By now you would think I've figured out how to
block out the noise
Build up walls of steel around my heart strong
enough to be bulletproof
Strong enough to shield me from you

I'd recognize that voice anywhere and I wish
time had given me the relief of forgetting you
 But like nails on a chalkboard, I still remember
your stupid dissonant whispers

It's been years, yet you still have the same
power over me
Fight, flight and freeze all at once every time I
see you

In the past, I so desperately wanted someone
who loves me to tell you off
Fight you for making me feel so helpless
Pull out their sword and put me behind them and
protect me
But we're older now and I don't have a prince
coming to save me from my demons

I will never let you know how much you've hurt
me
Give you that satisfaction
So I put on a brave face and go on with my day
like I don't even remember you
Pretend like I'm not shaking because we're older
now and I don't need anyone to protect me from
you because I can do it on my own

Stay

Spent my whole life thinking I had to keep
giving until I break
Thought I was impossible to love

Convinced myself that
when I finally climb that pedestal they'll want
me
They'll love me then

I spent years putting everyone else's needs
above my own
 Tried to hide my pain
Scared to say no
Didn't make a sound when it hurt
I was convinced no one liked me enough to stay
when the train slips off its track
Fake a smile so no one could tell how badly I
was breaking

Always first to apologize
First to send a pigeon and an olive branch
messages of hope, peace and love
Scared that if I didn't give it my all they'd walk
out

I don't need to string together excuses I can tell
you the truth
This is how it's supposed to be
No apologies for being who I really am

For some reason, you are not scared away by the
worst of me
Even when I fell off the pedestal
Thought I lost it all
You stayed

What Must It Be Like

I hate that look in your eyes
I could never read your mind
But I don't need x-ray vision to tell that you're
hurt

Never seen you lose your cool
But even heroes have their Achilles heels

Nothing shakes you
I've never met someone so brave
You'd fight a lion without weapons
Call that naive, but if anyone could win it would
be you
You look directly into the sun, that's just who
you are
Take it all on your own
I wonder what that must be like
Do you ever get tired?
Tired of always being strong

I could scream from the tops of mountains
Swim the oceans
Do whatever you wanted for me to prove my
love to you

But all of that would be useless if you didn't
notice
I'm asking if you'll let me be the one you lean
on when you need someone

Your skepticism breaks my heart
You push me away every time I just want to hold
your hand and tell you that you don't have to do
this alone

What is it like?
Closing yourself off from everyone, convinced
that it's not right unless you do it on your own
I guess you've been hurt before and you've built
these moats around the castles of your mind
Built walls so high up, I can barely see who you
are anymore
I don't know what else to do so I'm writing this
for you to let you know that I don't have any
hidden motives, I just want you to know it

I'll still stand by you, even if you push me away
a million times
Because for once I need you to see that life isn't
meant to be something you do all on your own
Please just take my hand to hold and know that
I'll do anything and everything to take the
weight off your shoulders

I'll let you see that there's strength in numbers
and sometimes asking for help is stronger than
facing it on your own

Please

Scared to love too quickly
No getting off this rollercoaster
One-way path to heaven or ruin
Dagger in your hand
Please carve me a statue made of love instead of
piercing through all the layers of my heart

I know one thing for sure
I can't repeat the same mistakes
So I'll pretend like I don't care
I'll wait hours before I reply
I'll act like I didn't spend the whole night
wishing you were mine

Fell for you faster than dust settles after a storm
I won't admit that you're always on my mind
Who am I to worry about you when I'm not
even yours

You say you just want to protect me
You're afraid you'll hurt me
I don't want to hear it
I hand you my heart and hope you don't shatter
it

I trace the black ink on your skin the way it laces
around your arm
You hold me close and whisper I love yous
 I just hope you know
you've written your name on my heart
I don't want to erase it
So please don't ruin this

Silence

Love is supposed to be worn with the brightest
colors
Matching outfits, and outlandish displays of love
I never wanted that
I just didn't want to be your secret
Someone you hide
Too afraid to show off to the light

I looked to your brown eyes
Didn't think it would end like this
and maybe it's my fault

Right person wrong time
Maybe that's what people say to make me feel
better

As I gave everything I had left to give
New Years, midnight kiss we filled the rooms
with laughter
Now all I hear is silence
 I'm tired of playing along
Lying to myself that you still want me

Do you really love me?
I want to be someone you're proud of

But here I am hidden and silenced
Looking out at you from the window
You look happier when I'm not next to you

I've never thought silence was a response
But here we are
And it's clearer than the bluest crystal clear
waters that I mean nothing to you

Right person wrong time
I don't think so
If you don't want me now, I know time won't
change that

If I hear right person wrong time one more time
I'll throw my broken heart out into the ocean and
hope a shark bites it and leaves me bleeding out
Maybe then I can feel something
Feel something more than this hurt you've left
me with

I'd give you all I can
Tried so hard to be what you needed
In the end it wasn't enough and it never will be
Because my love is just met with echoes of
silence

The One I Live For

I look at you and see your green eyes
Brighter than the prettiest emerald jewels on a
crown
How could anyone else ever compare?
You like me even when I hate myself

A love found once in a lifetime
I've heard it before and I'm sure you have too
I love you enough to die for you
What does that even mean?

It's true there are many people I love enough to
take a bullet for them
Stand in the rain with, face all their storms
together
Maybe I'd even kill for them
I'd do anything for them, but when it comes
down to it
who do I love enough to live for?

Actually, live for, not daydream about living
When the monsters under the bed come to say
hello
When the skeletons from the past open the closet
door hoping to destroy you

Who do you live for?

Is it the one who oozes honey with every word
they say
Swear they'd love you at your worst
Or is it the one that proves they love you with
every move they make
Who is it that you live for?
In the darkest moments when you think it's
better if you just run off and disappear
Who do you stay for?

I'll say it a million times
I stay for you, my love
I've never felt so strongly for someone the way I
do now
You lay next to me when I'm scared
You love me when I'm sad and I hope you know
I'd protect you and I'd find you in every crowd
My nightmares are all about losing you
Because when everyone says I'd die for you, I
know the only one I live for is you

Candles

A million candles
all whispering in the dark
little secrets they keep
There's a cake in the middle of all of it
Celebrations, new beginnings

A million thoughts racing
A million wishes I should be making
But I'm only thinking of you
Would you be proud of me if you saw me now
Or would you wonder where everything went
wrong

I look around when the party is over
No one's around and all I want is to not feel so
empty
I see you in the mirror
and I expect you to push me away
say that you've never been more disappointed
But you smile softly and you say
I know you're scared right now that everything is
going wrong
I know you feel like you haven't figured
anything out
But you survived all those storms

You saved yourself every time you fell down
And I believe in you enough to know that we
will figure life out one step at a time

So this time when I blow out the candles
I thank myself for holding on
I make no limits for my own dreams and I push
forward

Star-Crossed Lovers

I've walked down this dreary pebble road a
million times
Nothing new, nothing ever caught my eye
Until you came around and helped me see the
light

I'm too delusional to say that this is fate and just
move on
Maybe my head is in the clouds for thinking we
can change their minds
I'm too in love with you to say we're just
star-crossed lovers
A tragic tale, of love that faded away and leave
this all behind

If our red strings of fate are just parallel lines
I'll take all the threads and weave them together
to make you mine
We'll find a place where we don't have to be just
star-crossed lovers
Rewrite the stars and make them align

Run away with me
I'll meet you at the tidal basin
We can watch the sunrise

Have cherry blossom petals fall on us as we kiss
Write our own future as we embrace our past
and see that this isn't a story about star-crossed
lovers
In this story we end up together
It's perfect can't you feel it

In my dreams
You meet me out back
We take our horses and leave
Because differences in thinking, traditions,
religions, they're all excuses
to tear us apart
None of it would matter
But as much as I want us to be together forever
you say we're star crossed lovers, and no matter
how hard we try to change things we can't

I tell myself that if the multiverse is real, there's
a story where we end up together and we're not
torn apart by fate
One where Romeo marries Juliet and they live
happily
One where Jack survives and ends up with Rose
And one where we find each other and you're
brave enough to fight for us

The Moon and The Sun

Does the moon ever feel pride,
Knowing that when the sun makes its'
appearance
it always does so with a million colors filling up
the whole sky
Leaving imprints in the mind of those who see it
When it leaves it leaves with that same golden
glow

Does the moon ever hide behind the clouds, to
get a closer look at the sun
Captured by her beauty, stunned by her essence
Does the moon ever hope for longer moments at
dusk and dawn just for a chance to tell the sun
how much he loves her

You're the sun, the way you walk into a room
and not one person can turn away from you
The way you smile and all the planets wrap
around you
Left in a trance by your very essence
How could they not when you're handcrafted by
the heavens?

Am I foolish to think we have a chance?

To think that for once someone who's just like
the sun would fall for a girl filled with more
secrets than the dark side of the moon
That maybe for once it wouldn't be a story of
longing glances and playful conversations
But maybe something written in the stars that
lasted forever

The moon witnessed a lot of our stolen glances
I'd admire you from afar too scared to tell you
the thoughts that kept me up at night
Too afraid to send you that letter where I confess
my love for you
The moon was there when I'd talk myself to
sleep because you weren't around
The moon was there when you found me in the
rain and I told you I couldn't hide this anymore
The moon saw our secrets, our hidden
rendezvous, the dancing in your kitchen after a
long day
The moment you held my hand and told me that
you loved me with the same passion as the sun
at noon

And now we stand before the sun
In all our colors
No more longing glances
Because for once and forever I'm yours and
you're mine

With You

Maybe I've already met you, in a crowded
downtown street
Maybe we locked eyes for a sliver of time at the
cafe I go to every Wednesday
Maybe we met at the aquarium and brushed
hands as we went our separate ways
Maybe I saw you at the museum and instead of
looking at the history within the walls you
looked to me
Maybe I haven't met you yet, but when I do I
see a million different possibilities on how this
could go

You're sitting across from me
You order an iced americano and I'll order a
matcha latte with hints of lavender and thyme
And I'll be thinking of how nice it would be if I
got to call you mine

You take the brush and paint the sky the prettiest
colors
Blue like the dress I wore the day you first saw
me
Pink like the color my cheeks turn when you ask
when you'll see me again

I look to you as you sing every song just right

Even the smallest moments together feel like the definition of love

Is our love a butterfly that just emerged from a cocoon
Ready to fly and show the world all its' beautiful colors

Whisphers of I don't want this unless you are sure
Can this please be the last time I need to open up my heart
Can this be the last time I have to tell someone my story
The last time I ask someone if they believe in fate
Can this be the last first time

Can you be the one who shields me from all of lifes storms with your umbrella of love
The one who stays when things are falling apart
The one who holds my hand as I save myself
Can it please be you?

You're sure as you see me in that white dress
You joke that we'd make fate change its' plans if it tried to keep us apart, but I know you mean it
I know you'd find me in any lifetime
I'm not scared of eternity if it's with you

An Eternal Love

Dew drops on the leaves
Mist fills the thick summer air
I meet you there alongside the river
With you, I'm not afraid to be Icarus and touch
the sun

Captured by your beauty
Your skin sparkles like the glimmers of sunshine
so delicately meeting the ocean waves
The sound of your voice calms every fear of the
future
This must have been how Eros felt the first time
he saw Psyche

We meet under the trees
Soft grass beneath our feet as you braid my hair
with wildflowers
Even the heavens are envious of us in this
moment

With longing glances
Fleeting brushes of your fingertips on my arm
It is ecstasy that only comes when you're with
the right company

Like the moon lingers in the sky at dawn to get a
glimpse of the sun
I wait for you, and I admit that these feelings
aren't fading
They take root in my heart and they flourish
They wrap along each and every artery
Becoming my essence becoming my living force
and blood

Will you come to me?
Will we draw up a love story more passionate
than even Aphrodite and Adonis?
A love that is eternal, one where we can both
wear crowns of Helichrysum
Instead of separating and remembering our love
as fleeting and painfully beautiful like the
genesis of an Anemone

Our love will be one where we do not fear fate
because we believe in ourselves enough to know
that even when things go wrong we will pick up
the pieces and mend our love back together

Unending Infinities

We walked by the river
I've never seen the water sparkle just right,
clear, and calm
Just like my mind the night we first met
You're skipping rocks and making ripples in my
heart with every word you say
You pointed out the constellations in the stars
And I couldn't help but wish for a love
immortalized by the stars

You're crafting stories about mundane life but I
hold on to each word like it's magic
I've never felt so sure of anything
I hear the warnings
Something about promises of forever being
empty words
But with you, I know

I've heard it all before
Timezones, situations, distance
they're only excuses when you're not willing to
give it all you've got
With you I know

Like Perseus & Andromeda in the depths of my
heart I know
Even if we were worlds away, you'd find me
and bring me home safe
Nothing can keep us apart
I won't pay attention to the words against us
They call it blind faith but I'm willing to give
you everything I know

Even if I was chained to a rock
Locked away and seconds from my demise
Even if Cetus was in your way I know you'd go
to any lengths
Slay Medusa do anything you had to
Even if fire fell from the skies I know you'd find
a way to make sure that we'd be together
I believe in you enough to say this
I don't need stars or the sun I just want unending
infinities with you

Milton Keynes UK
Ingram Content Group UK Ltd.
UKHW050026250324
439966UK00014BA/954

9 789358 735222